MOTOR CAR

Other titles by Danny Byrne :-

Danny Gets to Grips with **Fishing**
Danny Gets to Grips with **Football**
Danny Gets to Grips with **Gardening**
Danny Gets to Grips with **Golf**
Danny Gets to Grips with the **Horse & Pony Care**

Danny
GETS TO GRIPS WITH THE
MOTOR CAR

STEP BY STEP
CAR
SERVICING
1 OPEN
BONNET

DC Publishing Paperback

Reprinted 1996

DC Publishing
11 Bryanston Village
Blandford Forum
Dorset DT11 0PR

First published 1995

Made and printed in Great Britain

for
ALL THOSE WHO DEARLY LOVE
THEIR MOTOR CAR

CONTENTS

FOREWORD

"We can all relate
to the scenes found in
this book. Danny has
cleverly translated everyday
situations into hilarious
happenings.

Each cartoon is complemented
by a few well chosen words to
leave us chuckling as we share
the joys of car ownership.

Happy Motoring !"

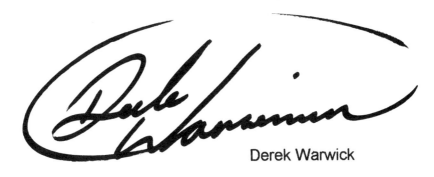

Derek Warwick

CAR PURCHASE....
General Information

There are ways of eliminating the
chance element of car purchase.

Whenever possible it's best to buy from
a recognised dealer.

Refrain from impulse buying.

Fuel consumption must be
taken into consideration.

With some makes of car
rust can be immediately apparent

Watch out for subtle signs of "car ringing".

If you buy privately, it's advisable to take
along an acknowledged negotiator for
additional purchasing power.

Don't overlook the mechanical soundness
of the car in favour
of the overall appearance.

When examining the bodywork, ask yourself
why someone would want you to view a car
under a makeshift shower.

Unscrupulous sales people can be persuasive.
Beware of unwanted extras.

Don't forget......You only get what you pay for.

SOME WORTHWHILE CHECKS
WHEN BUYING A
SECOND-HAND CAR

A small magnet is sufficient to check for
filler under the paintwork.

Check for evidence of
accident damage.

Check the upholstery.

Look under the vehicle for patches of
liquid on the ground.

Check tyres for signs of damage or wear.

Make sure there's a Jack in the boot.

Rough running may indicate more
serious problems.

Look for tell-tale signs of excess
oil consumption.

Smoke from the exhaust spells trouble.

On the test run check the brake response
before approaching a hazard.

Worn shockabsorbers can lead to a bumpy ride.

Make sure the car doesn't pull to one side.

You may wish to check insurance ratings
before deciding to buy.

SOME USEFUL TIPS WHEN SELLING A CAR

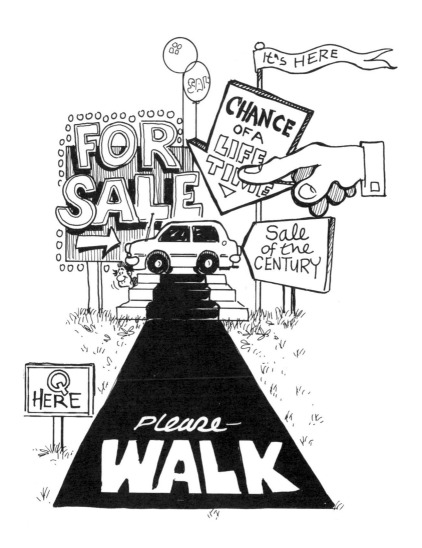

A tiny drop of shampoo will assist with a shine.

Detergent can leave streaks on the upholstery.

Be explicit, concise and low-key
with your advertising.

If negotiations start to break down,
resort to plan B.

Have all relevant documents ready for inspection.

First impressions are important, but there's
no point in trying to disguise any
major bodywork problems.

When a sale has been agreed, ask the buyer to
sign a paper confirming car has been
"bought as seen".

BASIC DRIVING TIPS & TECHNIQUES.

Being comfortable in the car produces
a relaxed driver.

Always drive at a safe distance from
the vehicle in front.

Keep up to date with modern roadsigns.

Always signal your intentions clearly and leave
no doubt in the mind of following drivers.

Never be bullied into driving
faster than you intend.

Air conditioning keeps the driver fresh and alert

When tired it's important to take a much earned
break before continuing your journey.

DRIVING IN BAD WEATHER

Expect the weather forecast to be a little
inaccurate occasionally.

Aquaplaning is always a danger during storms.

Boiling water gives instant visibilty when
applied to a frozen screen.

Limit your speed according to visibilty.

The thinking motorist is never caught out
by the weather.

A four-wheel drive will not aid braking.

Don't let bad weather put you off making
that special effort.

Stay at home if the weather is severe.

Share your journey plans with someone
before you leave home.

It's advisable to join one of the motoring
organisations such as the RAC or AA.

Snow tyres are available from most stockists.

BEATING THE CRIMINAL

Car theft can be reduced with a little thought
and application.

Try to get into the habit of removing the key
from the ignition.

Keep the ignition key in a safe place.

Concealing items of value deters
the casual thief.

Keep an eye on your car. If you have no garage,
leave it in a safe place.

If you go out at night and have to park your car,
do so in a well-lit area.

Where possible, park in a busy area.

Window etching can have unforseen drawbacks.

Sleep well....
Have a car alarm fitted.

D.I.Y. CAR MAINTENANCE

Simple maintenance can be managed
with the aid of a manual.

Mechanics mates should seek the appropriate
moment before retrieving their cutlery.

The multi purpose tool.

For the more advanced servicing jobs
you'll discover the need for other tools.

80

The quicker you can locate your tools, the
sooner you can start your service.

Always park your car on a firm, flat surface.

Do get help when lifting heavy parts.

Use a barrier cream
when attempting dirty work.

Brake pads may contain asbestos.

Home mechanics can take
minor maintenance to extremes.

Help from one's mate is always appreciated.

Home Tune is often an ideal alternative.

When confronted with niggling technical
problems, patience is the key.

A workshop can be a dangerous place for
young children.

When possible use manufacturer's
approved parts.

Keep a fire extinguisher handy at all times.

Never work on moving parts wearing
loose clothing.

If you intend to work alone, it's a good idea to
get someone to check up on you now and then.

Relax in the knowledge that you have saved
pounds by D.I.Y. car maintenance.